Genereris

PUBLISHING

The Contributions of Ghana's Minerals Resources to the Global Economy

Bauxite as a Case Study

Anamor Samuel Kofi

Title: The Contributions of Ghana's Minerals Resources to the Global Economy

Bauxite as a Case Study

ISBN: 979-8-89248-079-6

Author: Anamor Samuel Kofi

Cover image: https://pixabay.com/

Publisher: Generis Publishing
Online orders: www.generis-publishing.com
Contact email: info@generis-publishing.com

Authors

Anamor Samuel Kofi[1], Ahiahonu Desmond Senanu Loveridge[2], Nkansah Benjamin Oduro[3]

[1]Key Laboratory of Deep Coal Resource Mining, Ministry of Education of China, School of Mines, China

University of Mining and Technology, Xuzhou, 221116, China;

[2]Department of Architecture and Urban Planning, Chongqing University China

[3]School of Safety Engineering, China University of Mining and Technology, Xuzhou, 221116, China

Acknowledgments

We thank the ultimate God who created the universe for our entire being and the ability to structure this research. Expansionist the following individuals a responsibility of appreciation for their invaluable assistance: Professor Yuan Yong, School of Mines, at the China University of Mines and Technology in Xuzhou, China, Shayanowako Michael Kundai, PhD candidate of Mining engineering at China University of Mining and Technology, Xuzhou, China, Amartey Ernest Nii Laryea, PhD candidate of safety engineering and mining engineering, respectively, at the China University of Mines and Technology in Xuzhou, China.

Abstract

Empirical research shows that most African countries (for example, Ghana) are rich in natural resources and contribute their resources to the economic growth and development of the global economy. Ghana has valuable, semi-valuable, and industrial mineral resources—ideal geological and metallogenic conditions, policy orientation, and social and macroeconomic stability. Furthermore, the correlation analysis method combines information gathered from literary works with the co-authors' questions, the Supreme Court, administrative records, printed and digital sources discoveries on the factors and conditions of the mining process in the country. Which characterizes the intensity of mining production—calculating the correlation between each annual output based on the mining variables using several countries and mining communities' factors that were determined and utilized as the comparison sequence. Ghana's impact on the global bauxite mining industry cannot be overstated, given that the West African nation possesses some of the world's largest reserves of this restorative material. Ghana has significantly impacted the extraction, refining, and utilization of bauxite globally. According to the study's findings, Ghana's mining operations for bauxite and other minerals are predominantly concentrated in the Ashanti, Western, Northern, Eastern, and Central regions, with the Brong-Ahafo region used as the study's focus on the global economy. The research also investigates Ghana's ability to attract investors to utilize these abundant resources for world production and the potential implications of bauxite mining on a global scale. Adopting measures and technical solutions have been presented to decrease the effects of illegal mining on the Environment's damage and health risks in the mining zones.

Keywords: Ghana, Bauxite mining, Political, Mineral resources, Economy, Law, Investment.

Abbreviations

Abbreviations	Actual Meaning
CAGR	Compound annual growth rate
N.D.C.	National Democratic Congress
NPP	New Patriotic Party
G.D.P.	Gross Domestic Product
PNDCL	Provisional National Defence Council Law
RL	Reconnaissance Licence
PL	Prospecting Licence
ML	Mining Lease
RML	Restricted Mining Lease
GIADEC	Aluminium Development Corporation
IMF	International Monetary Fund
VALCO	Volta Aluminum Company
USD	United States dollar
G.B.C.	Ghana Bauxite Company Ltd
E.C.G.	Exton Cubic Group
NDPC	National Development Planning Commission
APNAC	African Parliamentarians Network Against Corruption
I.A.A.	Internal Audit Agency

Table of Contents

Chapter 1.

Introduction

1.1 Research Background

Ghana, located in West Africa, is renowned for its abundant natural resources, including bauxite, as depicted in Figure 1-1 to Figure 1-4 by country and others in the global mining arena in Ghana (2009 – 2021). Since the 15th Century, when Ghana was referred to as the "Gold Coast," mining has been an essential economic activity in Ghana. According to Global Data, Ghana is the eleventh most significant producer of bauxite in the world in 2022, and the country's production has increased by 31% since 2021[1]. Significant quantities of bauxite can potentially be found in both the state of Queensland and the state of Governor in Australia, which is the world's top mineral producer. Due to the country's significant mining industry, China is also the world's second-largest producer of bauxite behind Australia. Brazil, Indonesia, and India are among the leading countries that produce bauxite, along with several smaller countries. Guinea and Ghana are two countries in West Africa with significant bauxite reserves for their respective countries. Jamaica, Guyana, and Suriname are the three American countries subject to the continent's most extensive reserves. In the five years leading up to 2021, output in Ghana experienced a decline at a CAGR of decline of 13.18 percent[1].

However, it is anticipated that production in Ghana will increase at a CAGR of 1 percent between the years 2022 and 2026[1]. Ghana is Africa's second-largest gold producer after South Africa, and mining accounts for about 5% of the country's gross domestic product. Before independence in 1957, private foreign investors, mainly the British, dominated the mining industry. After independence, the Government established state-owned firms and bought existing mining concerns, shifting industry ownership. At the time of independence, the Government's primary purpose was to maximize state revenue and provide jobs for Ghanaians.

Ghana has established itself as a pioneer in responsible and effective bauxite mining. Ghana's importance in the global economy will expand as demand for this resource rises, from advancements in sustainable mining techniques to investments in local communities and infrastructure.

As a result, the state took ownership and control of its mineral resources, particularly the mining industry. From 1957 until the early 1980s, the state dominated the mining sector with minimal private engagement[2]. As previously stated, the state's purpose at independence was to manage the mineral resources, maximize state revenue, and create jobs. State-owned firms were, however, not treated with economic prudence or sustainability. The Minerals Commission oversees the exploration, development, and exploitation of mineral resources in Ghana's mining industry. The Commission guarantees that mining corporations comply with environmental and safety standards and fairly compensate communities impacted by mining activity. Ghana's mining industry has given the country advantages and difficulties. It has contributed significantly to the country's economic progress by providing jobs, generating funds, and attracting foreign investment.

Contrary to popular belief, mining is also responsible for environmental damage, societal strife, and human rights violations. Overall, the mining industry plays a vital role in Ghana's economy. Throughout the process, the Government is committed to ensuring that all stakeholders benefit from the process sustainably and responsibly.

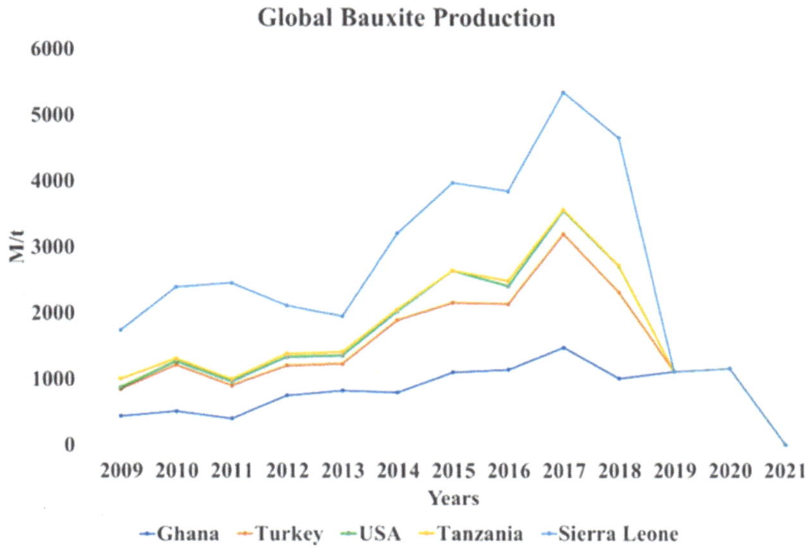

Figure 1-1 Global bauxite production[3].

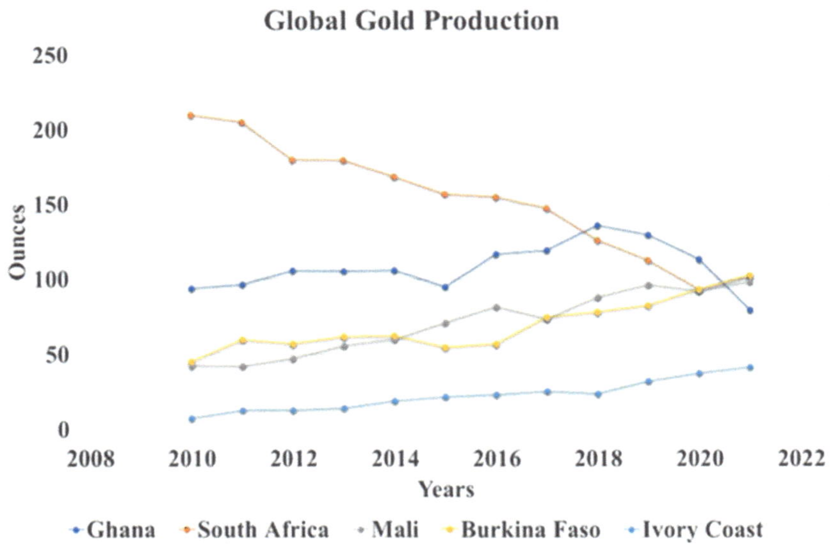

Figure 1-2 Global gold production[3].

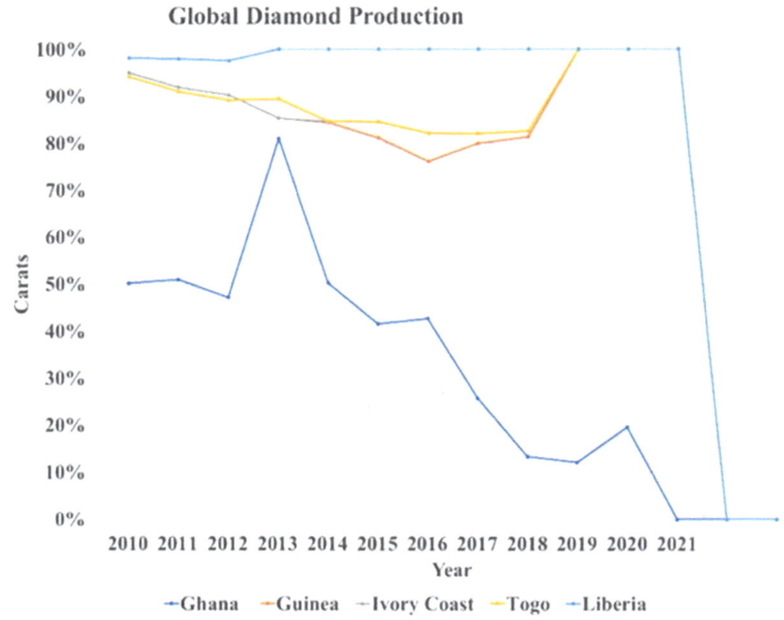

Figure 1-3 Global diamond production[3].

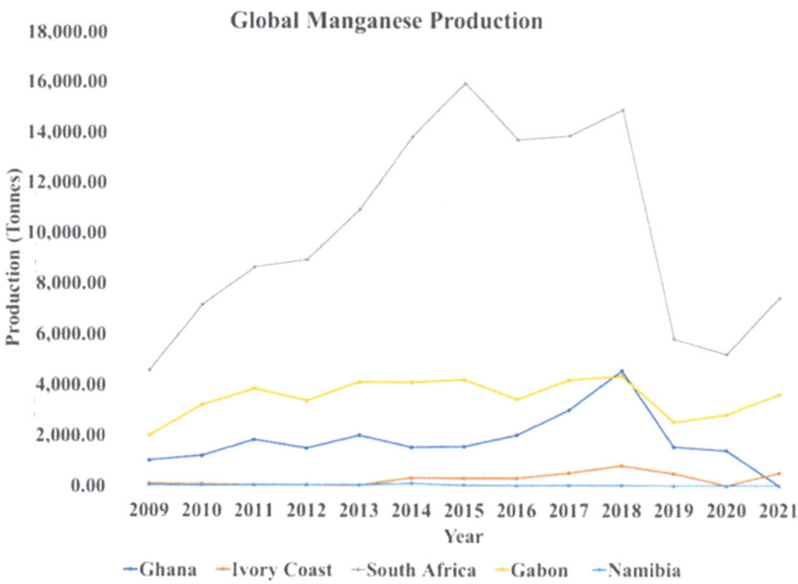

Figure 1-4 Global manganese production[3].

1.2 Significance of Study

The research and analysis of Ghana's mineral resources, specifically on bauxite and their contributions to the world economy, carries significant significance due to multiple considerations.

Ghana is renowned for its abundant mineral resources, and this research contributes to the comprehension of the revenue-generating potential associated with these minerals' resources, with a specific focus on bauxite. Bauxite is pivotal in manufacturing aluminum, a functional metal with extensive utilization across several industrial sectors. Through a review of the role played by Ghana's bauxite in the global economy, government officials and interested parties can assess the revenue-generating potential and prospects associated with this particular resource to obtain the information.

The practice of filling mining involves the application of waste materials to fill eliminates inside the locations of mines, including mining areas, subsidence regions, separation zones, and other vacant spaces within the mining environment. The primary objective of filling mining areas is to address the management of hazardous materials, including Bauxite residue (commonly known as red mud), tailings, and overburden. Additionally, it aims to regulate the movement of resources and mitigate surface subsidence, ultimately aimed at achieving the concept of "green mining"[4, 5]. The aims of bauxite mine filling and mining exhibit diversity. Certain mines are employed for green mining techniques to reduce the accumulation of waste materials on the surface. Conversely, others use technology to decrease the influence of underground pressure. However, the predominant objective is to extract gold from underground deposits and thereby extend the operational lifespan of the mine.

The relevant governmental ministries and commissions have established policy preferences on mining operations, including removing restrictions on the number of mining production sites and implementing policy measures to reduce taxes and provide incentives for mining reclamation. These initiatives align with the concept of green mining, as proposed in previous studies[6]. Fill mining technology has significantly improved as a crucial method for controlling surface deformation and implementing "three-down" pressured mining. The primary distinction among various filling technologies is the types of filling materials employed, the process equipment applied, and the degree of technological innovation implemented. Mineral material filling technique has demonstrated significant economic benefits, social benefits, and fill rate following extensive exploratory research and implementation by scientific research units and bauxite mining firms over several years.

In order to carry out the scientific outlook on development and support the transformation of economic development modes, the Ministry of Land and Natural Resources made the following recommendations in its guiding opinions on the effectiveness of the National Mineral Resources Plan, the development of green mining, and the construction of green mines. In addition to being a practical strategy for quickening the shift in the mining industry's development mode, it is a crucial tool that can promote company responsibility and industry self-discipline.

In compliance with the plans and specifications of the land and resources industry standards, the Ministry of Land and Natural Resources arranged for the appropriate departments to establish the suggested guidelines for the establishment of green mines in the non-ferrous, substance, gold, bauxite, sand, oil, diamond, cement, metallurgical, and nonmetallic industries. This is a public release following the standards' examination by the national technical committee to establish consistency of land and natural resources. Based on the fundamental requirements of green mine construction, mine environment, resource exploitation and application comprehensive usage of resources, energy savings and emission reduction, scientific and technological innovation, digital mines, and enterprise management, the national green mine construction specification is projected to be divided into nine major industries. These industries define the requirements primarily. The implication is that standard construction will be reached, and there will be a "law" to adhere to for Ghana's green mine building. A new era of green mine building in Ghana is anticipated due to the enforcement of these guidelines.

In mining bauxite, automation, intelligence, and information technology have replaced machinery as the standard. Furthermore, this is the only way to increase filling mining efficiency and achieve high output and efficiency using filling mining technology. Mining in Ghana has made an effort to implement mining filling technology in recent years. Still, the monthly output of mining filling has persisted due to several problems, such as inadequate equipment and a lack of automated control. This study functions as a means for the advancement of information and the exchange of optimal procedures among nations that possess comparable mineral resources. The structuring of global partnerships permits individuals or organizations to engage in information exchanges, leveraging from different perspectives, exploring innovative methodologies, and collaboratively addressing challenges about the extraction and usage of bauxite deposits.

The results of the study can contribute to the development of strategies at the governmental level. This framework has the prospect of presenting administrations with invaluable assistance in formulating measures that facilitate the widespread acceptance of environmentally-conscious mining methods, stimulate shareholders' attraction, and increase the financial benefits connected while improving the ecosystem and communicative drawbacks linked to bauxite mining.

The study of the economic contributions of bauxite mining on a global scale facilitates an in-depth study of the social and ecological repercussions associated with the mining and processing of this mineral's resources. This functions as the possibility to evaluate the sustainability measures implemented within the industry and determine techniques for decreasing any adverse consequences, including the destruction of forests, contamination of waterways, and movement regarding native collaborative environments.

This study aims to provide an understanding of the factors influencing foreign direct investment in Ghana's bauxite resources and its influence on the growth of the national economy. Understanding the effects of foreign direct investment in the mining industry is crucial for establishing initiatives and approaches aimed at recruiting extra investment, hence promoting economic expansion and facilitating employment opportunities.

Bauxite extraction processes generate employment and non-employment candidates to create advantageous results for the neighborhood residents and significantly contribute to addressing poverty. The in-depth study of Ghana's bauxite contributions to the global economy facilitates the understanding of authorities regarding the employment prospects associated with mining, thus enabling them to formulate strategies that enhance the generation of employment opportunities.

Ghana's bauxite resources can significantly contribute to the country's export revenue. Through an in-depth study of the role of bauxite in the global economy, governments can differentiate current economy structures, distinguish prospective export prospects, and discover opportunities for cooperation in order to strengthen Ghana's stance in the global economy and promote the advantages accrued from these valuable mineral resources.

Chapter 2.

Overview of Ghana

2.1 Geography

Ghana is a country in West Africa with a diversified geography of tropical rainforests, rolling hills, and sandy beaches. It has a total land area of around 238.53 square kilometers and over 31 million inhabitants. Each of the ten areas in Ghana exhibits distinct variations in geography and climate. The country in controversy is situated in the western region, sharing its western border with Cote d'Ivoire, its northern border with Burkina Faso, its eastern border with Togo, and its southern border with the Gulf of Guinea, as illustrated in Figure 2-1. The country lies between 4.5° and 11° N latitude and 3.5° W and 1.2° E longitude[7]. Two major physical zones dominate the landscape: the coastal plains in the south and the forested plateaus in the north. The coastal lowlands have sand beaches, lagoons, and mangrove swamps. Several rivers flow through the northern forested plateaus, including the Black Volta, White Volta, and Red Volta. Mount Afadja, 885 meters above sea level, is Ghana's highest point. The country's climate is tropical and humid, with two distinct seasons: The region undergoes a wet season extending from April to October, followed by a dry season from November to March. Ghana's location has had a significant impact on its history and culture. During the colonial period, the country's location on the coast made it a center for trade and business. The landscape diversity has also influenced the growth of many economic sectors, including agriculture, mining, and tourism.

Figure 2-1 Physical map of Ghana, equirectangular projection[8].

2.1.1 Political History

Ghana's political history dates back to the early 19th Century when European nations vied for regional dominance. In 1874, Britain seized possession and founded the Gold Coast Colony. In 1960, the colony achieved its independence and became the Republic of Ghana. Figure 2-2 depicts Kwame Nkrumah, Ghana's first president, who significantly influenced the nation's political structure. He advocated for Pan-Africanism and African socialism and implemented industrialization measures.

Figure 2-2 The renowned Pan-Africanist Kwame Nkrumah was Ghana's first president[9].

In 1992, after a succession of military coups, Ghana adopted a new constitution and returned to democracy. Since then, multiple democratic elections have been held, with power alternating between the (a) N.D.C. Emblem: The umbrella adorned with a bird's head at its tip, accompanied by the slogan "Unity, Stability, and Development[10]," and the emblem of the N.P.P., featuring a red, white, and blue background with an elephant positioned centrally, along with the slogan/motto "Development in Freedom[10]," as illustrated by the flags indicated in figure 2-2. The percentage of Ghana's G.D.P comprised mineral rents in that particular year was nearly negligible. The contribution of mineral rents to the G.D.P. in the preceding year amounted to approximately 1.8%[11].

Furthermore, it is worth noting that in 2011, the proportion of rents in Ghana's G.D.P. was nearly 5.5 percent[11], the highest percentage observed during the whole time under examination, as indicated in figures 2-3. A GDP per capita of over $2,200 in 2020 reflects the nation's substantial economic development over the past few decades.

However, Ghana continues to face several difficulties, such as extreme deprivation and corruption.

Figure 2-3 Two effective types of Ghanaian political flags: (a) N.D.C and (b) N.P.P[10].

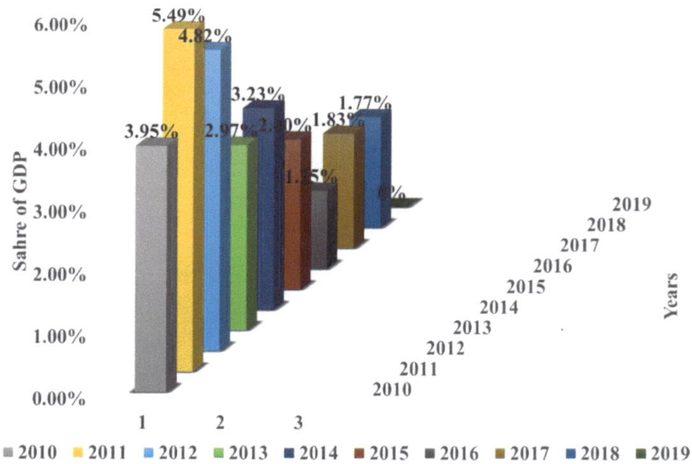

Figure 2-4 The percentage of Ghana's G.D.P. comprised mineral rents from 2010 to 2019[11].

Ghana's attempts to advance democracy and sound governance have recently attracted attention on a global scale. Aiming to diversify its economy and draw in outside capital, the nation has also emerged as a regional leader in producing cocoa, gold, and oil in Africa. Table 2-1 compares national per capita income based on the percentage growth rate and G.D.P. per capita.

Table 2-1 Compares the G.D.P., per capita income, and other economic indicators for different African nations[12, 13].

Country	Population	Nominal GDP(BillionUS$)	Per capita(US$)	Percentage Growth Rate(%)
Ghana	34,121,985	75	2,368	2.90%
Liberia	5,384,515	3.9	735	2.18%
Togo	8,806,874	8	960	2.52%.
Burkina Faso	22,465,443	18	824	2.55%
Zambia	19,785,797	27	1,348	2.76%
Nigeria	220,075,973	504	2,326	3.41%
Guinea	14,103,629	19	1,345	2.39%
Zimbabwe	15,452,140	38	2,420	2.11%
Ivory Coast	28,160,015	68	2,418	2.52%
Senegal	17,946,407	27	1,558	2.58%

Morocco	37,840,044	142	3,715	1.02%
South Africa	60,414,495	419	6,738	2.8%
Cameroon	28,647,293	44	1,584	2.63%
Niger	27,202,843	14	561	3.80%
Benin	13,712828	17	1,366	2.70%
Botswana	2,675,352	18	7,347	3.8%
Mali	23,293,698	18	857	3.10%
Sierra Leone	8,791,092	4	493	2.15%
Burundi	13,280,402	3.7	292	2.71%
Egypt	112,716,598	469	4,504	1.56%

2.1.2 The Economy of Ghana

The Ghanaian economy has experienced the fastest growth. It is one of the most stable and prosperous African countries, with a vibrant democracy, a peaceful coexistence of diverse ethnic groups and religions, and a strong respect for human rights and the rule of law. Over time, the nation has been able to maintain a macroeconomic environment that is reasonably stable, which has increased the number of foreign investments. Ghana's three main economic sectors are agriculture, mining, and services. Ghana's primary cash crop and source of a sizable portion of its export revenue is cocoa; the other significant resources the nation exploits are gold, diamond, limestone, and manganese. Despite the pandemic's impact, Ghana's economy is estimated to have grown in 2020 and is projected to rebound in 2021 and 2022.

In contrast to the investment inflow of 969.41 million U.S. dollars in 2019, as of 2021, Ghana's mining sector had attracted almost 1.1 billion U.S. dollars[11]. The investment inflows varied over the investigated period, reaching a peak in 2012 at 1.44 million dollars[11]. In March 2022, Ghana's mining and quarrying sector's producer price index was approximately 2,703[11]. The anticipated economic growth trajectory in 2023 suggests a deceleration and will remain depressed in 2024. However, the economy is anticipated to regain its potential development by 2025[14], as depicted in Figures 2-4 below. Ghana has also made remarkable progress in reducing poverty, from 52.6% in 1991 to 23.4% in 2016, and improving human development, ranking 133rd out of 189 countries in the Human Development Index[14, 15]. The Government will borrow a whopping ¢38.959 billion via treasury bills for the third quarter of 2023[16]. According to its issuance calendar released by the Ministry of Finance, this will be done via the issuance of the 91-day, 182-day, and 364-day bills[16]. The short-term debt instruments will be issued weekly to meet the Government's rising liquidity needs.

There have been positive developments in Ghana's economy, but several unresolved issues remain. These include a significant youth unemployment rate, inadequate facilities, and limited financing availability. In 2021, the producing member businesses of the Ghana Chamber of Mines were responsible for employing 12,236 individuals[17]. The current employee count represents a decrease from the previous year's 34,363 employees[18].

This information was considered in the statistical analysis of the prior year, as illustrated in Figure 2-4 below. According to the information provided by the source, slightly more than 99 percent of the workforce in the mining sector was composed of Ghanaians[11]. At the same time, the remaining employees were made up of foreign nationals. In 2021, the overall value of the country's mineral exports contributed somewhere in the neighborhood of 36 percentage points to the broad value of all export revenue[11]. The National Entrepreneurship and Innovation Plan, which offers grants and assistance to start-ups and small firms, is one of the Government's strategies to solve these issues.

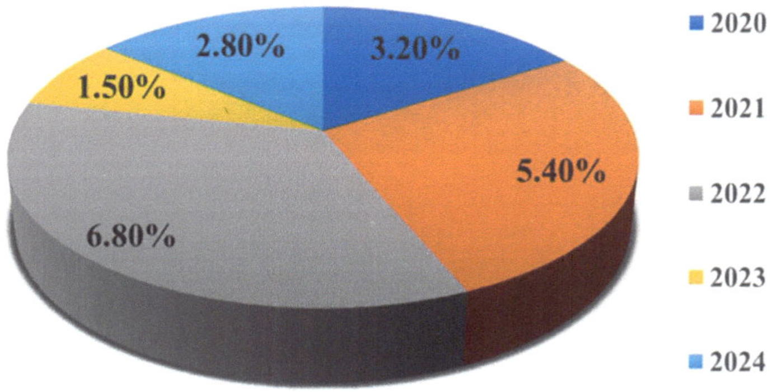

Figure 2-5 Ghana Recent economic developments[14].

As a result, agriculture, mining, and services have driven mainly Ghana's growth. Based on the contributions of minerals resources and the production and mining of bauxite resources in Ghana. The administration has implemented programs encouraging economic expansion, attracting foreign investment, and addressing economic problems. Ghana is well-positioned to continue its economic growth trajectory with ongoing infrastructure investment and adopting policies to address the financial issues.

2.2 Materials & Methods

Pertinent details concerning mining communities concerning international and national legislations, along with the types of transgressions committed by mining companies against these rights, will be acquired through an extensive exploration of relevant legal instruments, laws, and documents in libraries. Other sources, including the Supreme Court, various administrative records, and printed and digital sources, will be consulted. Shall rely on the experiences of mining communities, including observations and testimonials of particular mining community residents.

Chapter 3.

Mining Laws and Regulations in Ghana

3.1 Mining Investment Laws

The importance of mining investment legislation in Ghana has increased recently as the nation has seen growth in mining activities. Ghana has established various laws and regulations regulating mining activities to control and safeguard investors. The Minerals and Mining Act, 2006 (Act 703) and the Minerals and Mining (Amendment) Act, 2015[19], are two of these laws of particular importance. The Minerals and Mining Act, 2006 (Act 703) governs Ghana's mining industry. This law covers all aspects of mining, including site rehabilitation and the discovery and exploitation of minerals. Additionally, it creates the Minerals Commission as the regulatory agency in charge of regulating the nation's mining operations. The introduction of the Minerals and Mining (Amendment) Act in 2015 (Act 900) aimed to address problems that arose while implementing the Minerals and Mining Act of 2006[20]. This law aims to protect the Environment, encourage local participation in the mining industry, and provide for the confiscation of equipment used in unauthorized mining operations. The Minerals Development Fund Act of 2016 (Act 912), the Minerals Income Investment Fund Act of 2018 (Act 978), as amended by the Minerals Income Investment Fund (Amendment) Act of 2020 (Act 1024), and the Kimberley Process Certificate Act of 2003 (Act 652) are additional significant laws that govern mining[21].

In addition to these laws, mining companies operating in Ghana must abide by additional rules and regulations. Table 3-1 depicts that mining enterprises must get the necessary permits and licenses before commencing mining activities[22]. Additionally, they must follow environmental laws and use ethical mining techniques. Subsidiary law, as depicted in Figure 3-2, provides additional regulation relevant to many facets of the mining sector. The study presented in Figure 3-3 focuses on analyzing Ghana's government policy for preserving essential minerals. Simultaneously, the mining industry is subject to additional legal frameworks that pertain to the Environment, including the Environmental Protection Act 1994 (Act 490)[23] and its associated regulations.

Furthermore, other laws about natural resources, such as the Forestry Commission Act 1999 (Act 571), the Water Resources Commission Act 1996 (Act 522), and the Ghana Geological Survey Authority Act 2016 (Act 928)[21], along with their respective subsidiary legislation, also impact the mining sector. Others include the Local Governance Act of 2016 (Act 936), the Land Use and Spatial Planning Act of 2016, and the Lands Act of 2020 (Act 1036)[21]. The Companies Act, 2019 (Act 992), the Incorporated Partnership Act, 1962 (Act 152), the Ghana Investment Promotion Centre Act, 2013, the Income Tax Act, 2015 (Act 896), the Labor Act, 2003 (Act 651), and the Workmen's Compensation Act, 1987 (PNDCL 187)[21] are additional pieces of legislation that regulate the administrative elements of mining operations.

Table 3-1 The numerous mineral rights and licenses available in Ghana[22] .

License Type	Purpose	Area	Maximum Duration
R.L.	Regional exploration, not including drilling and excavation	Blocks of 21 hectares, not exceeding 5,000 contiguous blocks	12 months renewable
P.L.	Search for minerals and evaluation	Not exceeding 750 contiguous blocks	3 years, renewable with reduction of the area to not more than half
ML	Extraction of minerals	Not exceeding 300 contiguous blocks	30 years or less, depending on mine life. Renewable
R.M.L.	Building and Industrial minerals	Not exceeding 300 contiguous blocks	15 years or less, depending on mine life. Renewable
Small Scale Mining License (Reserve for Ghanaians only)	Extraction of minerals	In accordance with the number of blocks prescribed in Regulations	5 years, renewable

Table 3-2 Principal legislation and policies governing Ghana's mining industry[21].

A	B	C	D
Minerals and Mining (General) Regulations, 2012 (L.I. 2173)	Minerals and Mining (Support Services) Regulations, 2012 (L.I. 2174)	Minerals and Mining (Compensation and Resettlement) Regulations, 2012 (L.I. 2175)	Minerals and Mining (Licensing) Regulations, 2012 (L.I. 2176)

E	F	G	H
Minerals and Mining (Explosives) Regulations, 2012 (L.I. 2177)	Minerals and Mining (Explosives) Regulations, 2012 (L.I. 2177)	Minerals and Mining (Health, Safety and Technical) Regulations, 2012 (L.I. 2182)	Minerals and Mining (Ground Rent) Regulations, 2018 (L.I. 2357)

I	J	K
Minerals and Mining (Mineral Operations - Tracking of Earth Moving and Mining Equipment) Regulations, 2020 (L.I. 2404)	Minerals and Mining (Mineral Operations - Tracking of Earth Moving and Mining Equipment) Regulations, 2020 (L.I. 2404)	Income Tax (Minerals Income Investment Fund Exemptions) Regulations, 2020 (L.I. 2433)

Figure 3-1 Ghana's national policies on strategic minerals[24].

In essence, Ghana's mining investment laws aim to preserve the investors' capacity to operate in a consistent and foreseeable regulatory framework while safeguarding the country's and its citizens' interests. These laws and regulations will probably change as long as Ghana's mining sector continues to expand to keep the industry viable and advantageous for all parties involved.

3.2 Mining Act 2006 (Act 703)

Aiming to control and manage the development of Ghana's natural resources, the new Minerals and Mining Act 2006 (Act 703)[25] also addresses issues about acquiring mineral rights, the Environment, public health and safety, land usage, and community relations. The Act outlines laws for the ownership of minerals, the forced purchase of land for mining purposes, the application for mineral rights, and the reservation of land from mining. It also establishes the Minerals Commission as the primary regulating agency for the mining industry. The Act also includes provisions for safeguarding public health and safety, preventing environmental deterioration, and advancing the welfare of mining communities[26].

3.2.1 The Influence of Government on Mineral Amendments Holders

The Ministry of Lands and Natural Resources and the Minerals Commission administrate Ghana's mining industry. The Minerals Commission was created per the Minerals Commission Act 1993 (Act 450)[27, 28] to fulfill its legal mandate of overseeing and controlling the exploitation of natural resources and harmonizing the associated regulations[28]. As part of a mining lease, the Minister of Lands and Natural Resources may enter into a stability agreement with the holder to ensure that the holder is not the entity in concern had negative consequences as a result of subsequent modifications to the magnitude and distribution of royalties, revenues, charges, and other fiscal imports. Consequently, plant, machinery, equipment, and accessories imported mainly and solely for the mining operations are exempt from paying import duties, and a personal remittance quota that is exempt from the tax that is imposed by an act that regulates the transfer of funds out of the country for expatriate staff. A stability agreement cannot exceed fifteen years and must be ratified by the legislature.

Chapter 4.

Ghana Bauxite Mining Zone

4.1 Bauxite Deposits

Ghana is a prominent bauxite supplier to China, possessing substantial reserves and exhibiting outstanding mineral grades, as depicted in Figures 4-1 to 4-2. As indicated in Table 4-1 to 4-2, the majority of Ghana's bauxite deposit areas, such as the Western Province's Afo-Sefwi Bekwai (Awaso), the Ashanti Province's Aya Nyinahin, the Eastern Province's Atewa Range (Kibi), and the Eastern Province's M.T. Ejuanema. The Western Province's Afo-Sefwi Bekwai (Awaso) region has granted mining rights to the G.B.C. Bauxite reserves were first uncovered in Ghana's Awaso region in 1921. Ghana's primary bauxite deposits are in Awaso, Kibi, M.T. Ejuamena, and Nyinahin. Ghana's bauxite reserves are estimated to amount to 554 million metric tons, with the Awaso deposit actively producing and exporting predominantly to Europe since 1942. According to Achiaw, Ghana's refinery and bauxite deposits can yield 1.5 to 2 million tons of alumina annually.

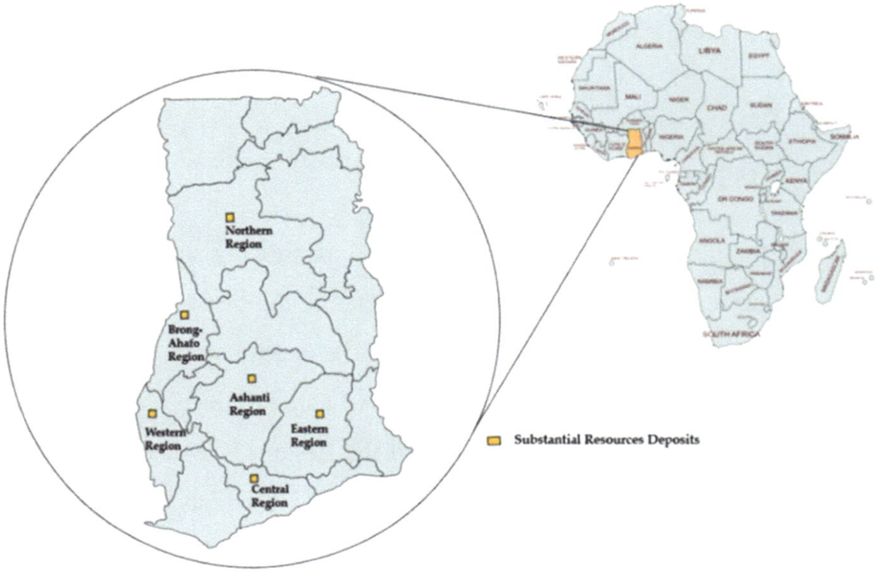

Figure 4-1 Map distinct substantial resources deposits region of Ghana.

1940, the Ghana Bauxite Corporation was established, following the mining authorization granted to the British Aluminum Company in 1928. In 1974, the Ghanaian Government acquired 55% of the business, making it the largest stakeholder[29, 30]. In 1982, Alcan bought Britannia Aluminum. The Ghanaian Government sold Alcan its 45 to 80% holding in G.B.C. in 1988[31], giving it an 80% stake in Ghana's bauxite and elevating Alcan to its most significant shareholder position[32]. Rio Tinto acquired Alcan before the end of 2007, and the business was renamed Rio Tinto Alcan. In February 2010, Chongqing Bosai Mining Group Co., Ltd. acquired all of Rio Tinto Alcan's shares, making it a significant shareholder.

Ghana's largest bauxite mine is the Aya Nyinahin one in Western Province. E.C.G. received the mining permit from the previous administration. Following the shift in the governing party, the mine has faced numerous legal disputes and challenges. Residents and environmental organizations have hampered it at the same time. Nationalizing mining rights is a top priority for the present administration. No individual or organization received the remaining two tenements. Tema or Secondi-Takoradi are the destinations for transporting bauxite for processing because of the pre-existing infrastructure in these cities, including docks and rail networks.

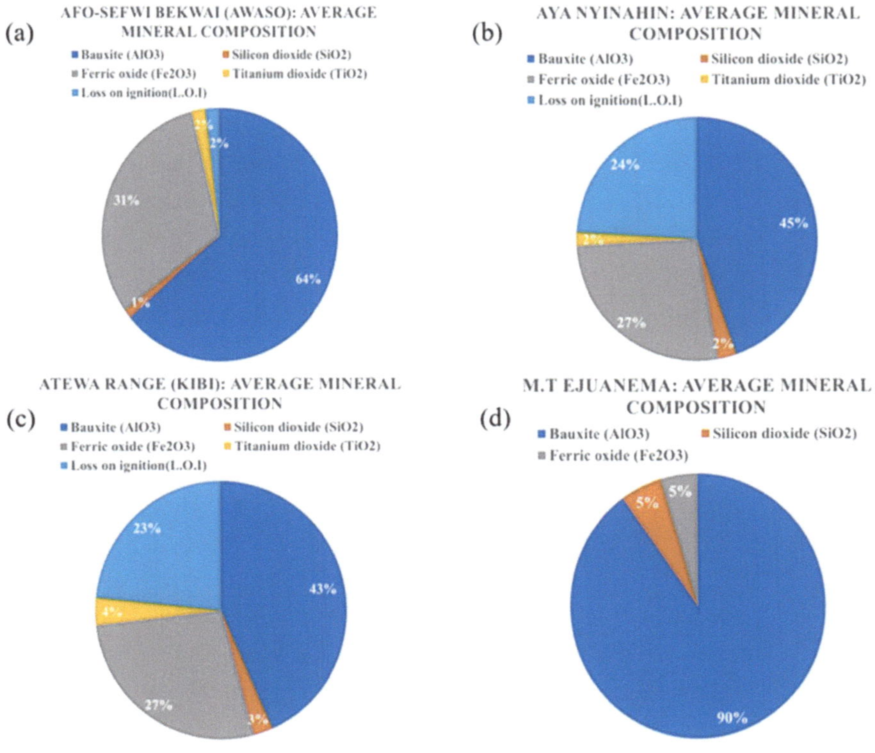

Figure 4-2 illustrates Ghana's estimated reserves and average mineral composition of significant mining areas: (a) Afo-Sefwi Bekwai (Awaso) 19 reserves (million tons) (b) Aya Nyinahin 350 reserves (million tons) (c) Atewa Range (Kibi) 180 reserves (million tons) (d) M.T Ejuanema 5 reserves (million tons).

Table 4-1 Larger Mining Areas in Ghana.

Destination	Region
Obuasi	Ashanti Region
Iduapriem (Tarkwa)	Western Region
Damang	Western Region
Prestea /Bogoso	Western Region
Wassa	Western Region
Kenyasi	Brong-Ahafo Region
Akyem	Eastern Region
Chirano	Western Region
Teleku Bokazo, Nzema	Western Region
Ayanfuri	Central Region
Amansie West	Ashanti Region
Kwabeng	Eastern Region
Osino	Eastern Region
Awaso	Western North Region
Nsuta	Ashanti Region

Table 4-2 Smaller Mining Areas in Ghana.

Destination	Region
Odumpara Bepo	Eastern Region
Nkwanta Bepo	Eastern Region
MT. Kwakwati near Akwadum	Western Region
Range of hills trending	Western Region
Northwards from M.T Kwantama	Eastern Region
Range of hills between Asempaneye and Pomakrom	Western Region
Kwamisa Bauxite Deposite	Ashanti Region
Range northeast of Awuakrom	Ashanti Region
Kansiri Hill near Edubia	Ashanti Region
Mpuasu Hills	Brong Ahafo Region

Chapter 5.

Current Bauxite Mining Situation

In Ghana, industrial-scale mining for bauxite and other solidified minerals started in the 1970s. Bauxite mining is currently in an adequate state, nevertheless. Numerous issues have plagued the nation, including social unrest, environmental deterioration, and an ineffective government. Based on the findings of the Ghana GIADEC report, it is projected that the bauxite deposits in Ghana amount to around 900 million tons[33], with an estimated refined value of $400 billion[34]. The amount of bauxite that Ghana produced in 2020 was over 1.16 million metric tons[35], an increase from the previous year's production of approximately 1.1 million metric tons[11]. The amount of bauxite mined in the country experienced substantial fluctuations, with output reaching its highest point in 2017 at roughly 1.5 million metric tons[11]. In light of the recent negotiations about the Atiwa bauxite mining project, including the Chinese, it has been determined that the Chinese party is entitled to a 5% share of the bauxite reserves, estimated at 20 billion.

The administration of the New Patriotic Party (NPP) has expressed its intention to utilize Ghana's bauxite resources to secure a financial injection of $2 billion from China[36], which would be allocated towards various developmental initiatives. The Minority in Parliament has also lodged a petition with the I.M.F. about the matter. I.M.F. has issued a cautionary statement regarding the potential for China to gain control over Ghana's mineral resources as a result of outstanding loan obligations. As per the report, China will be granted the authority to utilize the revenue generated from Ghana's oil, cocoa, bauxite, and electricity sales for debt settlement.

Over almost two decades, Ghana has procured a total loan amount of nearly $5 billion from a minimum of 41 credit facilities provided by the People's Republic of China[37,

38]. The nation can generate up to 10 million tons annually with the correct investments in exploration and infrastructure (such as roads and trains).

There have been some constructive advances in recent years. The Government has taken action to solve some challenges, and community support for sustainable mining techniques is growing. The Government of Ghana holds a 20% equity stake in the mine, and China's Bosai Minerals holds the remaining 80%[39, 40]. Through the Takoradi Port, all the bauxite produced is shipped to China in concentrate form.

Currently, the mine cranks out a little over a million tonnes of bauxite annually. To help Ghana become an integrated producer of aluminum, VALCO was founded. For the VALCO facility, Ghana does not have a domestic smelter to convert bauxite into alumina. As a result, all of the alumina processed at VALCO comes from abroad. VALCO now has an annual capacity for refining aluminum of around 60,000 metric tons[41]. This will be increased as part of the integrated aluminum program to 300,000 metric tonnes[42, 43]. The Ghanaian Government is considering ordering a feasibility study to see whether constructing a domestic smelter would be economically viable. However, much more effort must ensure that Ghana's bauxite mining sector is sustainable and profitable for all parties involved.

5.1 Bauxite-Related Policies and Export Prices in Ghana

Mahamudu Bawumia, the vice president of Ghana, is dedicated to utilizing the nation's vital natural mineral resources, such as bauxite, to accelerate the country's rapid economic development. Bauxite mining provided Ghana with revenue of 22 million dollars in the United States in 2021[11]. This resulted in a decline in revenue compared to the previous year, with 37.72 million United States dollars recorded[11]. A total of 50.89 million United States dollars was made from bauxite sales in 2017, whereas only 11.16 million United States dollars were made in 2009. Figure 5-1 represents the maximum and minimum revenue generated from bauxite sales for the specified period.

As of the beginning of March 2022, the price of a metric ton of bauxite in Ghana was approximately 54 dollars in the United States. A license must be obtained from the Minister of Lands and Natural Resources to export, sell, or dispose of a mineral. The granted license is not assignable. The Government recently established the Ghana Bauxite Committee, presided over by the Ghana Minerals Committee, to enhance bauxite development and export management[44]; it intends to present legislation in Congress to establish the Ghana Bauxite Aluminum Comprehensive Development Authority: Rough mineral imports and exports are governed by the Kimberley Process Certificate Act, 2003 (Act 652)[45]. A Kimberley Certificate must be provided by the Minister or another individual designated by the Minister to anyone planning to export a specific raw mineral resource.

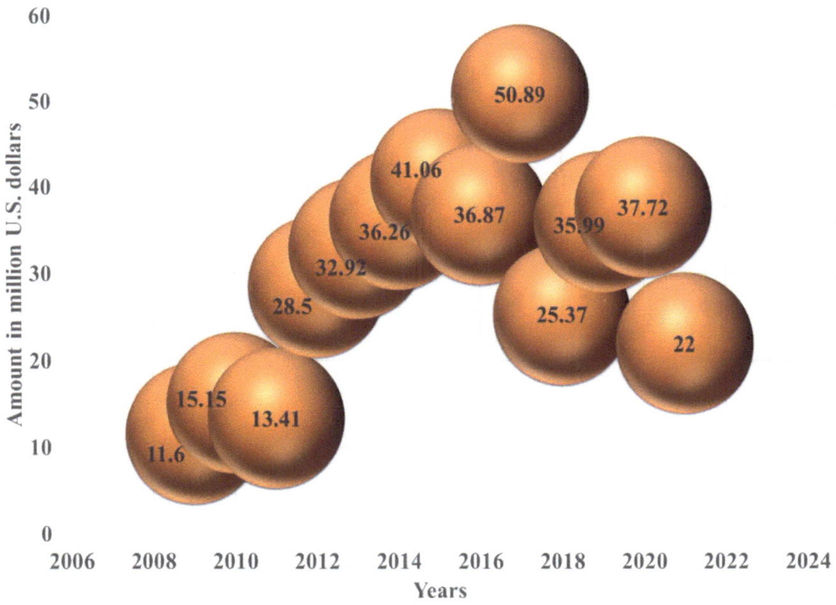

Figure 5-1 Revenue generated by the Ghanaian Government from bauxite mining in Ghana between 2009 and 2021, expressed in millions of U.S. dollars[11].

The Government also plans to switch from exporting unprocessed bauxite ore to a whole industry chain with deep processing and preliminary refinement. The Government of Ghana plans to employ a consulting company to investigate the nation's bauxite reserves thoroughly. The Ghanaian Government won't issue bauxite mining permits until the exploration is complete.

In contrast, the Ghanaian Government encourages people and companies to submit declarations of intent for cooperation and detailed plans on bauxite resources in advance. Currently, the Government wishes to collaborate in two key directions. The first is that investors will invest in the mining and refining of bauxite. The distribution of the revenues will be 55% (negotiable)[2]. The corporate income tax liability for mining operations amounts to 35%[46, 47] of the chargeable income generated from such operations during each assessment year.

In order to determine the taxable income derived from the mineral activities of an individual, each distinct mineral activity is regarded as a separate entity for assessment. The business's tax burden is computed autonomously for each fiscal year of evaluation. In exchange for mining rights, the Government must construct the necessary infrastructure. The current export price of bauxite is $400 per ton [48], the cost of initial processing is between $800 and $1,200 per ton [49], and the cost of final processing is $1,900 per ton [50].

5.1.1 Bauxite Mining in Ghana and its Effects on the Environment

It frequently calls for strip mining of topsoil, which calls for removing any remaining forest cover. The Atewa forest is a vital ecosystem, according to the World-Wide Fund for Nature, and environmentalists are concerned that bauxite mining can cause permanent damage to the area. A truck carrying 10 tonnes of mining explosives collided with a motorbike on January 20, 2022, along the Tarkwa-Bogoso-Ayamfuri road in Western Region, Ghana, causing a significant explosion. 300 km west of Accra, the explosion destroyed the adjoining Bogoso-Appiatse hamlet, killing 13 people and wounding 200 others. Authorities stated that 500 buildings were destroyed in the blast, displacing over 500 individuals, as shown in Figure 5-2, after further research. Subsequent investigations established that the supplier of the explosives was in breach of the regulations governing the manufacture, storage, and transportation of explosives.

Due to the gravity of the incident, the company was handed an administrative fine of $1 million, exceeding the statutory limit of $10,000.

In addition, the company was ordered to reimburse the Ghana Cedi equivalent of $5 million to the Government[21]. Following research, it was determined that the supplier of the explosives had violated the regulations that regulate the manufacture, storage, and transportation of explosives in violation of those regulations. The severity of the incident resulted in the organization receiving an administrative fine of one million dollars, significantly more than the statutory maximum of ten thousand dollars. In addition, the corporation was ordered to submit to the Government an amount equivalent to 5 million U.S. Dollars in Cedi.

Figure 5-2 Devastation brought on by the explosion in the Prestea Huni Valley Municipality's Appiatse village, located on the Bogoso-Bawdie route. (The provided images are credited to Bestshowbiz, Norvanreports, and Reuters).

Additionally, the rate of deforestation in West African nations increased by 60% in 2018 compared to 2017[51]. Global Forest Watch figures show that much destruction occurred inside protected areas. Deforestation has terrible effects. In Ghana, the agricultural sector accounts for around a third of all jobs. These farmers have endured drought and temperatures as high as 43 degrees Celsius (109 degrees Fahrenheit), which scientists have linked to climate change brought on by deforestation because tropical forests release water and control air temperature. According to Ghana's Ministry of Environment, Science, Technology, and Innovation, rainfall has decreased by 20% over the past few decades due to climate change.

5.2 Negotiations between the Ghana government and enterprises

Figure 5-3 shows an agreement of cooperation with China Railway that was signed in June 2017 during the visit of Mahamudu Bawumia, the vice president of Ghana, to China. The agreement covers projects totaling about $2 billion. In May 2017, the Ningxia Tianyuan Manganese Industry Group and the Vice President of Ghana signed a memorandum of cooperation on the development of bauxite.

Figure 5-3 On June 22, 2017, a meeting occurred in Beijing, China, between Chinese Vice President Li Yuanchao and Ghanaian Vice President Mahamudu Bawumia. (The provided images are credited to Xinhua and Ding Lin).

Following the statement made by Honorable George Mireku Duker, the deputy minister for Lands and Natural Resources with oversight on the mining industry. Figure 5-4 represents how the 21st ADU meeting transpired in Perth from September 6–8, 2023, according to its standard framework that featured live presentations, practical debates, and opportunities for business networking[9]. The delegation included Mr. Martin Ayisi, the CEO of the Minerals Commission, and H.E. Samuel Yao Kumah, Ghana's High Commissioner to Australia, along with additional high-profile figures. The event was held in the Pan Pacific hotel in Perth, excluding participation from African regions.

During his keynote speech at the Meeting, Hon. George Mireku Duker, the deputy minister, emphasized the enduring stability of Ghana's democratic system, its significant mining cultural significance, and the ongoing exploration and identification of valuable mineral resources. This contains Lithium and other essential minerals that perform a vital role in the clean energy initiative. The deputy minister also emphasized the presence of a solid legal and administrative mining framework in Ghana, contributing to its status as the foremost investment opportunity for mining destinations in Africa.

Figure 5-4 Hon. George Mireku Duker, Ghana; participating in a panel discussion alongside Hon. Bill Johnston, Australia's Minister of Mines; Hon. Tim Watts, Australia's Assistant Foreign Minister; Hon. Simon Pierre Boussim, Minister of Mines and Quarries, Burkina Faso; Hon. Henry Dele Alake, Minister of Solid Minerals Development, Nigeria; and Hon. Ruth Nankabirwa Ssentamu, Minister of Energy and Minerals Development, Uganda. (The provided images are credited to MLNR).

Chapter 6.

Additional Significant Minerals in Ghana

Figure 6-1 depicts that Ghana's mineral resources include gold ore, diamond, manganese ore, iron ore, limestone, bauxite, oil, and gas. According to Figure 6-2, the mineral production in Ghana for 2020 amounted to approximately 14.04 million metric tonnes, encompassing various minerals such as precious metals, iron, and ferro-alloy metals[11]. This was a minor drop in production compared to the output recorded the year before. As a result of the increasing amount of mining that is being done in Ghana, this nation is now recognized as one of the most significant producers of minerals like manganese in all of Africa. In the 1980s, Ghana began to privatize and divest itself of its assets, including by welcoming foreign investment into its mining industry, which had previously been state-owned. American Newmont Goldcorp, Chinese, Canadian, South African, and Australian mining enterprises are among the largest in Ghana.

Figure 6-1 Six different types of mineral resources. (a) Gold ore (b) Diamond (c) Bauxite (d) Manganese ore (e) limestone (f) Iron ore (Source: Modified from different online website).

In its attempts to foster economic growth and development, the Government of Ghana has designated the mining industry as a priority area of attention. The Ministry of Lands and Natural Resources is working to grow the sector by establishing a Mining Development Fund, among other initiatives. This fund will finance exploration, mining operations, and infrastructure development. Ghana has made considerable strides in strengthening its mining industry in recent years. Existing mines expanded, and several new mines developed. The country is currently home to some of the largest gold mines in Africa, including the AngloGold Ashanti-operated Obuasi mine.

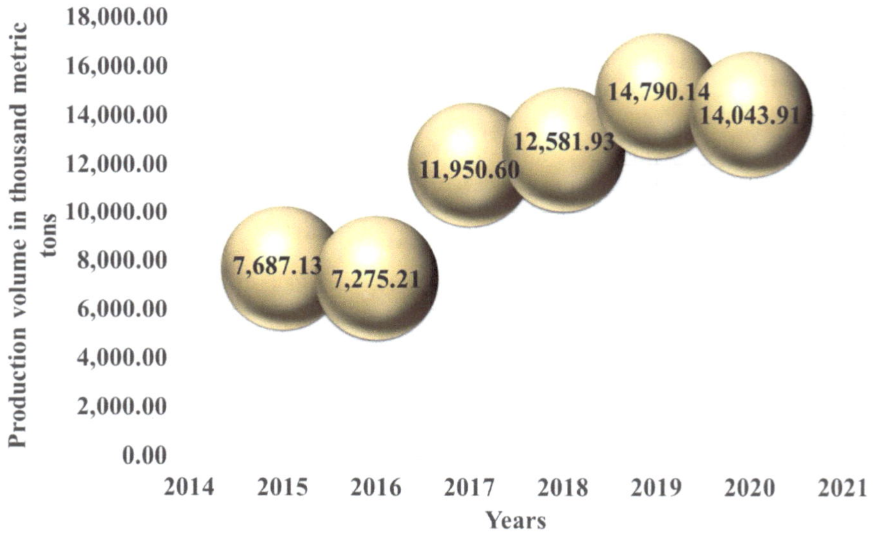

Figure 6-2 The present study examines the production volume of minerals in Ghana over five years, specifically from 2015 to 2020[11]. The data is presented in metric tons, with values expressed in thousands.

6.1 Exploitation of Ghana's Natural Resources

The effective management of Ghana's natural resources presents a variety of beneficial and detrimental implications for the country as a whole. The achievement of Ghanaian citizens' expectations requires to be guaranteed in the management of the country's natural resources. As shown in Figure 6-3, Inadequate land management practices cause the landscape to degrade and generate annual deforestation costs of US$400 million and an economic strain of over US$500 million[52, 53]. Ghana has diverse, abundant assets, including minerals, ecosystems, natural gas, and oil deposits.

Additionally, the dedicated and intelligent use of these resources can contribute to global economic expansion, employment creation, and growth in infrastructure. However, it is essential to practice cautious management to prevent adverse social and ecological implications from their exploitation. Five million land areas of forest were destroyed during the period from 2001 to 2015.

Figure 6-3 The contributions of illegal mining and inadequate land and forest management to improving the Environment are currently significantly impacted.

In the ten years that have followed, Figure 6-4 to Figure 6-5 present the practice of traditional gold mining has contributed to the deterioration of environmental degradation, mainly through the excavation of waters such as rivers and streams such as Birim, Ankobra, Pra, Densu[54, 55], and others have experienced pollution due to the detrimental effects of unauthorized mining activities in the river systems, including those within the Atewa Forest region, beyond the boundaries of the Ashanti region in search of deposits.

Figure 6-4 The presence of illegal gold miners in Ghana has resulted in unregulated mining activities causing significant pollution in rivers in the Eastern, Western, and Ashanti regions. (A) The Birim River is situated in the Eastern region. (a) The present state of the Birim River in the Eastern area. (B) The Ankobra River is situated in the southwestern region of Ghana. (b) The modern-day course of the Ankobra River, which flows across southwestern Ghana. (The provided images are credited to Modern Ghana, Kwesi Yankah, GHEnvironment, and GhanaWeb).

Figure 6.5 The presence of illegal gold miners in Ghana has resulted in unregulated mining activities causing significant pollution in rivers in the Eastern, Western, and Ashanti regions. (C) The Pra River is situated in south-central Ghana (c) The present state of the Pra River is located in south-central Ghana (D) The Densu River is situated in the South Eastern part of Ghana (d) The present state of the Densu River is located in the South Eastern part of Ghana. (The provided images are credited to Modern Ghana, Kwesi Yankah, GHEnvironment, and GhanaWeb).

6.1.1 Challenges

Illegal mining, which makes up much to 30% of the nation's total gold production, is one of the biggest problems. Illegal miners frequently work without adhering to appropriate safety and environmental standards, which can result in environmental degradation and health risks. A further factor impeding the sector's development is a lack of investment. This restricts access to high-quality ore deposits and prevents the expansion of existing mines, as evidenced by the limited reserves at the Nauli 377 (million tons), Buipe 20.5 (million tons), Bongo Da 15 (million tons), and Oterkpalu 13.2 (million tons) mines, as depicted in Figure 6-3. As illustrated in Figure 6-4, the reserves at Himakrom total 5.46 million tons, Aketechi 0.81 million tons, Odumasi 1.705 million tons, Kapili Hill 17.31 million tones, Kalimbi Hill 14.33 million tons, and Nsuta 1.45 million tons. Oppon Mansi 150 reserves, as depicted in Figure 6-5 (million tons). Figures 6-6 to Figure 6-7 illustrate the Sheini 27 reserves (million tons) and the Pudo 4.5 reserves, respectively.

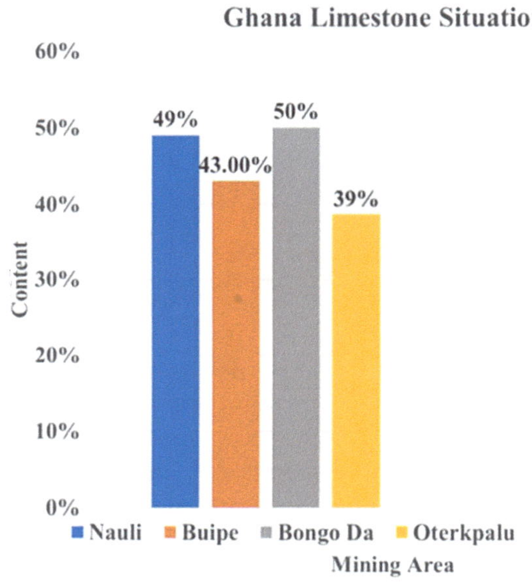

Figure 6-5 Limestone mining area situations.

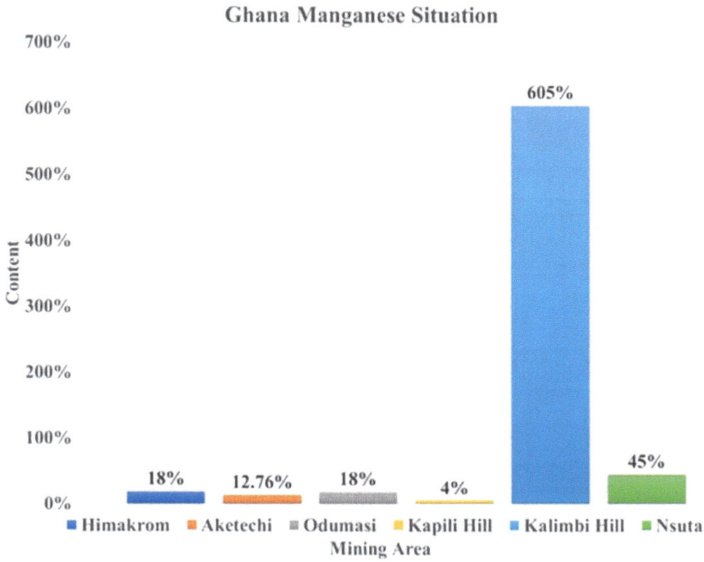

Figure 6-6 Manganese mining area situations.

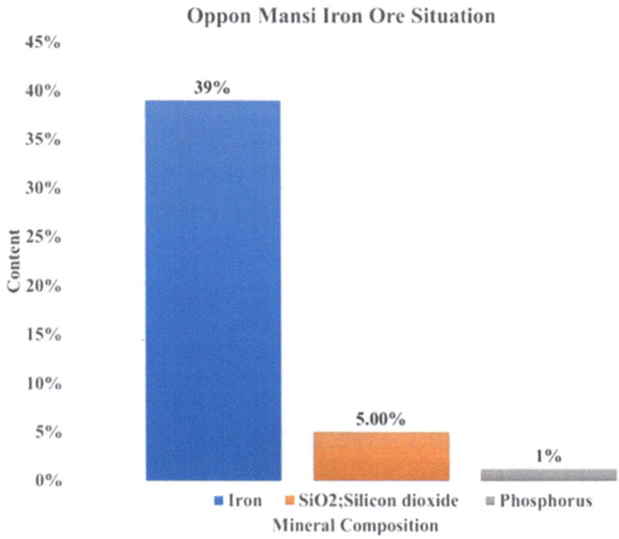

Figure 6-7 Iron ore mining area situations.

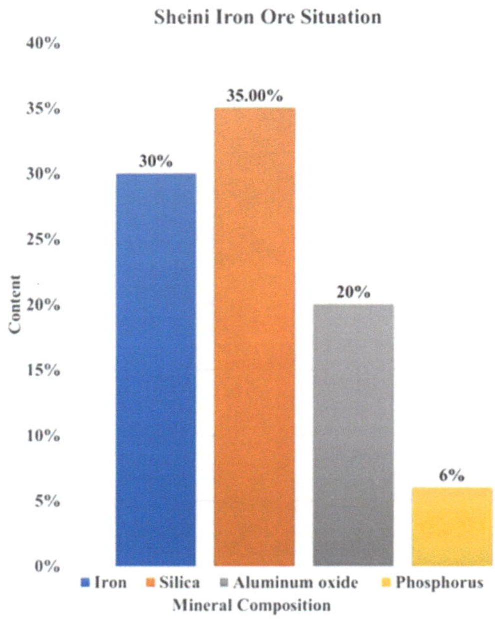

Figure 6-8 Iron ore mining area situations.

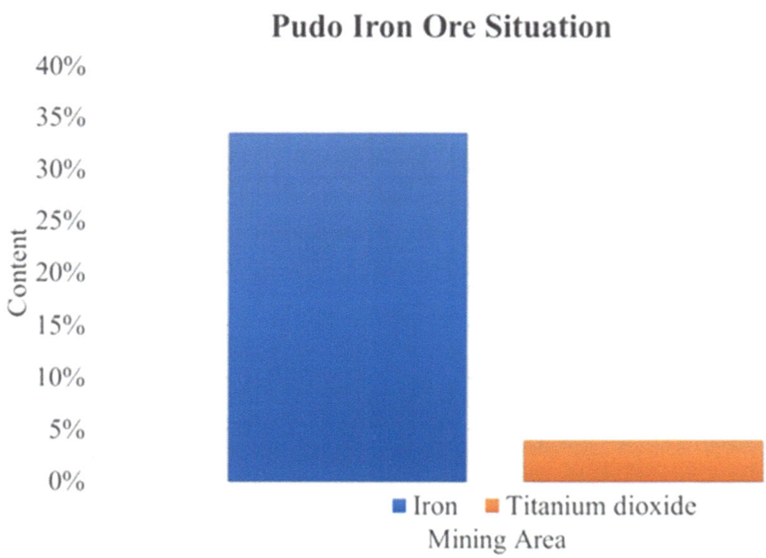

6-9 Iron ore mining area situations.

6.2 Utilization of Ghana's Capacity

Ghana possesses substantial bauxite resources and has implemented proactive measures to foster the growth of its aluminum sector. Furthermore, the country boasts a conducive business environment, making it an appealing aluminum industry investment hub. On September 14, 2021, several significant initiatives were inaugurated under H. E. Nana Addo Dankwa Akufo-Addo, the President of the Republic of Ghana, as part of his agenda. The inauguration ceremony was attended by Hon. Samuel A. Jinapor, Hon. Alan Kyeremanteng, and other prominent personalities, as depicted in Figure 6-8. The initiatives, which are currently begun by the Ghana Integrated Aluminium Development Corporation (GIADEC), aim to optimize the usage of Ghana's bauxite deposits. The proposed initiatives encompass the enlargement of the current mining operations in Awaso, the establishment of a new mine in Nyinahin-Mapasaaso, and the construction of a refining facility.

As mentioned, the initiatives include establishing a mining operation in Kyebi, a secondary mining operation in Nyinahin-Mpassaaso, constructing a refinery, and enhancing the Valco smelter through modernization and enlargement. These endeavors aim to enhance operational efficiency and augment production capacity. The announcement of Rocksure International, an indigenous Ghanaian company, to achieve a significant milestone by being selected through a highly competitive bidding process involving 39 companies contending for the project. This selection positions Rocksure International as the leading entity responsible for spearheading the development of the bauxite deposit and implementing a refinery solution. A contractual agreement was executed between Rocksure International and GIADEC, representing the Government of Ghana.

The execution of the agreement will facilitate GIADEC in commencing mining activities within 24 months. Additionally, a refinery solution is expected to be developed within four years. The success of the projects would rely on the presence of 900 million tonnes of bauxite reserves located in three specific regions of the country:

Awaso in the Western North Region, Nyinahin in the Ashanti Region, and Mpasaaso in the Eastern Region. As mentioned earlier, President Akufo-Addo asserted that the initiatives hold significant importance in pursuing the Ghanaian Government's agenda of achieving self-reliance and reducing dependence on foreign assistance, also known as the Ghana Beyond Aid Agenda. The individual expressed a steadfast dedication to developing a prosperous Ghana, emphasizing that the Act of signing the agreement demonstrated the governing party's commitment to fulfilling their promises to the Ghanaian people. The individual asserted their unwavering confidence in the credibility of Rocksure International as a prospective partner for GIADEC. The President emphasized that GIADEC, regarded as the future metal, should be promptly and efficiently carried out by the Board and Management.

Figure 6.10 The acts of His Excellency Nana Addo Dankwa Akufo-Addo launching four aluminum development projects[56].

The Minister for Lands and Natural Resources, Samuel A. Jinapor, stated that the GIADEC has made significant progress in fulfilling President Nana Addo Dankwa Akufo-Addo's commendable and ambitious vision since its establishment around two and a half years ago. The individual expressed that the Government, through means of the Ministry, has implemented extensive measures to facilitate the efficient and accountable use and conservation of the nation's natural resources. The GIADEC aims to utilize Ghana's current bauxite reserves and associated aluminum assets to facilitate the comprehensive commercial utilization of the country's bauxite reserves. This will involve refining bauxite into alumina and further smelting alumina to produce aluminum. Additionally, GIADEC will promote the growth of downstream industries to enhance the aluminum sector's value-added potential.

6.3 Results & Discussion

Despite these challenges, there remains tremendous potential in Ghana's mineral production industry. The nation has enough bauxite for aluminum production. The Government of Ghana should eliminate all security forces from mining concessions[57], examine any mining-related incidents involving state security forces, and punish those responsible.

Effective implementation of region-specific content and collaboration in regulations and guidelines constitutes an essential requirement for ensuring that the general population derives value across the whole mining chain of production, originating from the pre-feasibility stage, followed by prospecting, research (such as projects focused on environmentally sustainable mining science and technology, including the application of intelligent technology for robotics and automation and cleaner extraction techniques) advancement, and concluding with advertising and mine settlement.

Additionally, there are measures to cease the exports of bauxite and iron ore in their unprocessed form shortly—the Government's policy to retain the country's highest end of the mining value chain. As per the statements made by Nana Addo Dankwa Akufo-Addo, the President, the most effective approach to maximize the advantages derived from our natural resources involves enhancing their worth through value addition and establishing sufficient connections with other sectors of the economy. If Ghana's mineral-based sector addresses illegal mining concerns and attracts more investment, it can significantly contribute to economic growth and development.

In order to construct integrated aluminum and iron and steel sectors in the nation, the Ghana Integrated Aluminum Development Corporation (GIADEC) and the Ghana Integrated Iron and Steel Development Corporation (GIISDEC) were established. In addition, a fund to established to support the construction of mining settlements, and legislation to enacted requiring mining enterprises to provide social amenities such as schools and health facilities.

Conclusion

In conclusion, it is abundantly evident that Ghana's existing mining state for bauxite and other solid minerals possesses significant potential. This sector can potentially boost Ghana's economy if planned and invested properly by government institutions such as NDPC, APNAC Fundo Minerals, I.A.A., and others. These initiatives must incorporate more effective means of financing exploration efforts and improving infrastructure to use these resources effectively. In addition, environmental restrictions must be considered while formulating strategies for upcoming developments; there is no denying that Ghana gains a great deal from its mineral wealth.

Summary

The country of Ghana, in concern, ranks as the third most significant contributor to bauxite production within the African continent to the global economy. Furthermore, Ghana holds the difference of being the second-largest producer of gold in Africa. However, over several decades, the range has experienced degradation as a result of the enduring impacts of forest management, health risk, harvesting operations, and the reclamation of agriculture-related lands in conjunction with the establishment of bauxite and other significant mining operations within the Atewa forest and surrounding areas. Despite the country's persistent efforts, it has not yet achieved the goal of turning this priceless commodity into an operational generator for social and economic progress. As a result, this book analyzes the administration, including its responsibility, legal framework, governmental structure, primary functions, policy formulation, global cooperation, and aims, among other factors. It implements techniques and leverages technological innovations to mitigate the adverse ecological effects of illegal mining activities throughout mining regions.

References

[1] **Bauxite production in Ghana and major projectsGlobalData** [https://www.mining-technology.com/data-insights/bauxite-in-ghana/?cf-view]

[2] Akabzaa T, Darimani A. Impact of mining sector investment in Ghana: A study of the Tarkwa mining region[J].*Third World Network,*2001, 11(2).47-61.

[3] MINES TGCO. **MINING INDUSTRY STATISTICS AND DATA**. In, 2020 edn. 44.

[4] Liu T, Lin B, Yang W, *et al.* An integrated technology for gas control and green mining in deep mines based on ultra-thin seam mining[J].*Environmental Earth Sciences,*2017, 76.1-17.

[5] Li L, Xu LJ, Chen DM. Connotation and technology system of green mining of manganese resources[J].*Advanced Materials Research,*2013, 734.540-545.

[6] Kilu RH, Afutu-Kotey RL. Mining in Green Technology Space: Perspectives of Multinational Mining Companies in Ghana[J].*Journal of Business Research,*2017.

[7] Addi M, Asare K, Fosuhene SK, *et al.* Impact of large-scale climate indices on meteorological drought of coastal Ghana[J].*Advances in Meteorology,*2021, 2021.1-17.

[8] **Regions Of Ghana Map** [https://www.worldatlas.com/maps/ghana]

[9] **Attending the Africa Down Under (ADU) conference?** [https://ghana.embassy.gov.au/acra/ADU2019.html]

[10] **About Ghanian political party flags** [https://www.crwflags.com/fotw/flags/gh%7D.html]

[11] **Production volume of minerals in Ghana from 2015 to 2020(in 1,000 metric tons)** [https://www.statista.com/statistics/1270176/production-volume-of-minerals-in-ghana/]

[12] **List of African countries by GDP (nominal)** [https://en.wikipedia.org/wiki/List_of_African_countries_by_GDP_(nominal)]

[13] **South Africa GDP 1960-2023** [https://www.macrotrends.net/countries/ZAF/south-africa/gdp-gross-domestic-product]

[14] **Poverty Reduction in Ghana: Progress and Challenges** [https://www.worldbank.org/en/country/ghana/publication/poverty-reduction-ghana-progress-challenges]

[15] **Ghana maintains medium human development but inequality remains – UNDP** [https://www.ghanabusinessnews.com/2022/09/11/ghana-maintains-medium-human-development-but-inequality-remains-undp/]

[16] **Government To Borrow A Whopping ¢38.959bn Via T-Bills In Quarter 3** [https://www.theghanareport.com/government-to-borrow-a-whopping-%C2%A238-959bn-via-t-bills-in-quarter-3/#:~:text=Government%20will%20borrow%20a%20whopping,day%20and%20364%2Dday%20bills.]

[17] Donkor P, Siabi EK, Mensah SK, *et al.* Developing an Improved Strategy for Addressing Environmental Issues Caused by Artisanal and Small-Scale Mining (Asm) in Ghana[J].*Available at SSRN 4389593.*

[18] Kanu IA. Environmental and Socio-Economic Impact of Mining on Operational Communities in Tonkolili District Northern Sierra Leone[J].*Journal of Civil Engineering Research & Technology,*2022, 4(2).1-7.

[19] Eshun PA. Fiscal Policy Reforms and Their Effects on the Economic Viability of Mineral Projects in Ghana[J].*International Journal of Economics and Finance,*2018, 10(8).64-76.

[20] Arthur-Holmes F, Busia KA, Yakovleva N, *et al.* Artisanal and small-scale mining methods and the Sustainable Development Goal 6: Perceived implications for clean water supply[J].*Environmental Science & Policy,*2022, 137.205-215.

[21] **Mining Laws and Regulations Ghana 2023** [https://iclg.com/practice-areas/mining-laws-and-regulations/ghana]

[22] **Type of Mineral Rights** [https://www.mincom.gov.gh/mineral-rights/]

[23] Mensah AE, Justice A, Osei ON, *et al.* Does Environmental Laws and Policies Work? A Review Of Ghana's Case[J].*Research in Ecology,*2020, 2(3).32-41.

[24] Acheampong DT. **The Energy Transition and Critical Minerals in Ghana: Diversification Opportunities and Governance Challenges**. In. 2022. 90.

[25] Ali-Nakyea A, Amoh JK. Have the generous tax incentives in the natural resource sector been commensurate with FDI flows? A critical analysis from an emerging economy[J].*International Journal of Critical Accounting,*2018, 10(3-4).257-273.

[26] Adu-Baffour F, Daum T, Birner R. Governance challenges of small-scale gold mining in Ghana: Insights from a process net-map study[J].*Land Use Policy,*2021, 102.105271.

[27] Tenkorang EY. Illegal Small-Scale Mining in Asutifi North District, Ghana: Traditional Authority's Tacit Support for an Illegality[J].*African Social Science Review,*2021, 11(1).7.

[28] Bird N, Avoka C. Budget support, aid instruments and the Environment: the country context[J].*Ghana country case study Final Report London: ODI and Accra: CDD-Ghana,*2007.

[29] Pereira V, Tuffour J, Patnaik S, *et al.* The quest for CSR: Mapping responsible and irresponsible practices in an intra-organizational context in Ghana's gold mining industry[J].*Journal of Business Research,*2021, 135.268-281.

[30] Opintan-Baah E, Yalley P, Kwaw P, *et al.* **An investigation into the activities of the Environmental Protection Agency (EPA) in the Ghanaian construction industry: a case study of Sekondi-Takoradi Metropolis**. In *WEST AFRICA BUILT ENVIRONMENT RESEARCH (WABER) CONFERENCE 19-21 July 2011 Accra, Ghana 2011.*2011.131.

[31] Hendrixson KL. **Seeking the economic kingdom: The impact of state majority ownership of the Ghana Bauxite Company on company performance**. Fletcher School of Law and Diplomacy (Tufts University). 1989.

[32] Ménascé D. Special Issue 14| 2016 Environmental and social acceptability of major industrial projects: from risk management to shared prosperity[J].

[33] Acheampong T. The Energy Transition and Critical Minerals in Ghana: Diversification Opportunities and Governance Challenges[J].2022.

[34] **Ghana promotes local content after discovery** [https://www.miningweekly.com/print-version/ghana-promotes-local-content-following-bauxite-discovery-2021-04-02]

[35] Gurmendi AC. The mineral industry of Spain[J].*Minerals Yearbook,*2007, 3.25.

[36] Adom AY. **Analysis of the role of foreign donor aid in Ghana's economic development and povery alleviation**. 2015.

[37] Brautigam D, Hwang J. **Eastern promises: New data on Chinese loans in Africa, 2000 to 2014**. In. Working Paper. 2016.

[38] Foster V. **Building bridges: China's growing role as infrastructure financier for Sub-Saharan Africa**, vol. 5. World Bank Publications. 2009.

[39] Darimani A. Preliminary research report and list of activities[J].2013.

[40] Purwins S. Same Same, but Different: Ghana's Sinohydro Deal as Evolved' Angola Model'?[J].*Insight on Africa,*2023, 15(1).46-70.

[41] Andreini M, Giesen N, Edig A, *et al.* **Volta Basin water balance**. In. ZEF discussion papers on development policy. 2000.

[42] Barnafo AO. The development of Ghana's aluminium industry[J].1983.

[43] Husband C, McMahon G, Veen Pvd. The Aluminum industry in West and Central Africa: Lessons learned and prospects for the future[J].2009.

[44] Tsikata FS. The vicissitudes of mineral policy in Ghana[J].*Resources Policy,*1997, 23(1-2).9-14.

[45] Antwi F. **An assessment of the impacts of Newmont Gold Ghana Limited (NGGL) on the Socio-Economic Development after six years of Operation in the Birim North District**. 2010.

[46] Kusi NK. Tax reform and revenue productivity in Ghana[J].1998.

[47] Asa E. Comparing alternative mineral taxation systems for gold mining in Ghana[J].*1990-1999-Mines Theses & Dissertations,*1994.

[48] Agbolosoo EK. **Mineral processing in a less developed country: Bauxite processing in Ghana**. The University of Arizona. 1991.

[49] Opoku L, Gyimah AG, Addai B. Harnessing waste-to-energy potential in developing countries: a case study of rural Ghana[J].*Environmental Science and Pollution Research,*2022, 29(38).58011-58021.

[50] Fluctuation P. Vulnerability of Artisanal and Small Scale Mining to Commodity[J].

[51] Odijie ME. Sustainability winners and losers in business-biased cocoa sustainability programmes in West Africa[J].*International Journal of Agricultural Sustainability,*2018, 16(2).214-227.

[52] Eswaran H, Lal R, Reich P. Land degradation: an overview[J].*Response to land degradation,*2019.20-35.

[53] Stanturf JA, Mansourian S. Forest landscape restoration: state of play[J].*Royal Society open science,*2020, 7(12).201218.

[54] Asamoah E. **The impact of small scale gold mining activities on the water quality of River Birim in the Kibi traditional area**. 2012.

[55] Kuffour RA, Tiimub BM, Agyapong D. Impacts of illegal mining (galamsey) on the Environment (water and soil) at Bontefufuo area in the Amansie West district[J].*J Environ Earth Sci,*2018, 8(7).98-107.

[56] **PRESIDENT AKUFO-ADDO LAUNCHES FOUR ALUMINIUM DEVELOPMENT PROJECTS** [https://mlnr.gov.gh/index.php/president-akufo-addo-launches-four-aluminium-development-projects/]

[57] Hilson G. Shootings and burning excavators: Some rapid reflections on the Government of Ghana's handling of the informal Galamsey mining 'menace' [J].*Resources Policy,*2017, 54.109-116.

www.ingramcontent.com/pod-product-compliance
Lightning Source LLC
LaVergne TN
LVHW051130210926
848482LV00001B/44

* 9 7 9 8 8 9 2 4 8 0 7 9 6 *